THIS IS THE JOURNEY OF...

_____

_____

_____

"DON'T JUDGE ME
BY MY SUCCESS,
JUDGE ME BY
HOW MANY
TIMES I FELL
DOWN AND GOT
BACK UP AGAIN."

-Nelson Mandela

ESTABLISHING DISCIPLINE WITHIN
YOURSELF IS GUARANTEED TO
ENHANCE YOUR LIFE IN MANY WAYS.
USE THIS GUIDED JOURNAL AS
A HELPFUL TOOL TO TAP
INTO YOUR TRUE POTENTIAL.
LET IT GUIDE YOU TO DISCOVER
AREAS OF IMPROVEMENT, HELP YOU
BUILD AND BREAK HABITS,
WITH MOTIVATIONAL
QUOTES AND POSITIVE AFFIRMATIONS
TO ENCOURAGE YOU ALONG THE WAY.
BLESSINGS ON YOUR JOURNEY.

Day 1

Set your intentions: What habits would you like
to break or build from this experience?

Be Mindful

Day 1

Be Mindful

Day 2

What are you willing to give up to accomplish your goals?

Day 2

Day 3

It's time to commit! Lets set a routine.
Remember: Those days you feel like giving up,
are the ones most important to conquer.

Day 3

Day 4

Use the following 7 pages to self reflect.
Where do you see yourself after this journey?

Go Hard Or Go Home

Day 5

Day 6

Day 7

Day 8

Day 9

Day 10

You Against You

Day 11

You Against You

"ON THE ROAD TO ACHIEVING YOUR DREAMS YOU MUST APPLY DISCIPLINE. BUT MORE IMPORTANTLY CONSISTENCY, BECAUSE WITHOUT COMMITMENT YOU'LL NEVER START, BUT WITHOUT CONSISTENCY YOU'LL NEVER FINISH."

-Denzel Washington

YOU ARE DOING INCREDIBLE! THIS IS A REMINDER TO FORGIVE YOUR SELF FOR ANY MISTAKES OR TIMES YOU'VE FALLEN SHORT ON YOUR JOURNEY.

It's Time To Lock Back In!

Day 12

Now that you are on the path of discipline,
what have you learned about yourself so far?

Self Discovery

Day 12

Day 13

Do you feel more in control of yourself?
If no, why not?

Practice Self Control

Day 13

Practice Self Control

Day 14

What changes have you noticed about yourself?
How have these changes benefited your life?

Day 14

Day 15

What are you most grateful for in your life?

Take a Breath

Day 15

Day 16

Prepare yourself for your next milestone.
In what areas of life do you need more discipline?

Day 16

Day 17

Challenge #2
Break at least 1 bad habit and build 1 good habit.
Use the next 30 pages to reflect on your journey.

Use these prompts to help guide your reflection:

These are the steps I've been taking
to break/build my habits. . .

Spend some time outside, then journal
how you feel afterwards.

Why have you chosen to stop certain bad
habits that also make you feel good?

Meditate & Focus

Day 18

Day 19

The Grind

Day 20

Day 21

Day 22

Day 23

Day 24

Day 25

Day 26

Day 27

Day 28

Day 29

Day 30

Day 31

Day 32

You're halfway through your second challenge.
What's working for you?
What do you need to adjust?

"YOU'RE CLOSER TO WHERE YOU'RE TRYING TO GET THAN WHERE YOU STARTED FROM."

-Nipsey Hussle

Day 33

Day 34

Day 35

Day 36

Day 37

Day 38

Day 39

Day 40

Day 41

Day 42

Day 43

Day 44

Day 45

Day 46

Day 47

"MOTIVATION GETS YOU GOING, BUT DISCIPLINE KEEPS YOU GROWING. THAT'S THE LAW OF CONSISTENCY. IT DOESN'T MATTER HOW TALENTED YOU ARE. IT DOESN'T MATTER HOW MANY OPPORTUNITIES YOU RECEIVE. IF YOU WANT TO GROW, CONSISTENCY IS KEY."

-John C Maxwell

TAKE A DEEP BREATH.
YOU'VE COMPLETED
THE 30 DAY CHALLENGE!
HOW DO YOU FEEL?
TAKE THIS TIME TO
SELF REFLECT ON HOW
FAR YOU'VE COME.

Day 48

Contemplate on the bad habits you broke.
How did you accomplish this?

Day 48

Day 49

Contemplate on the good habits you've built.
How did you accomplish this?

Day 49

Enjoining The Good

Day 50

Do you believe you are developing discipline?

Day 51

What have been your biggest struggles thus far?

Faith Over Fear

Day 51

Faith Over Fear

Day 52

Finish the sentence: I am. . .

Day 53

Who do you look up to?
What traits about them do you admire?

Learn From The Finest

Day 54

How can you take those traits you admire
and integrate them into your journey?

Implementation

Day 55

Final Challenge
Break at least 3 bad habits and build 3 good ones.
Use the next 60 pages to track your progress.

Challenge Time

Day 56

Conquer Yourself

Day 57

Day 58

Conquer Yourself

Day 59

Day 60

Conquer Yourself

Day 61

Day 61

Conquer Yourself

Day 62

Conquer Yourself

Day 63

Day 64

Conquer Yourself

Day 65

Conquer Yourself

Day 66

Day 67

Conquer Yourself

Day 68

Day 69

Day 70

Day 71

Day 72

Day 73

Conquer Yourself

Day 74

Motivation Check:
How closely are you sticking to your routine?
If you're not, it's time to get back on it today!

Conquer Yourself

"EVERY MORNING YOU HAVE TWO CHOICES: CONTINUE TO SLEEP WITH YOUR DREAMS OR WAKE UP AND CHASE THEM."

-Carmelo Anthony

"EVERY MORNING
YOU HAVE TWO
CHOICES CONTINUE
TO SLEEP WITH
YOUR DREAMS OR
WAKE UP AND
CHASE THEM."

Carmelo Anthony

Day 75

Conquer Yourself

Day 76

Conquer Yourself

Day 77

Day 78

Conquer Yourself

Day 79

Conquer Yourself

Day 80

Day 81

Conquer Yourself

Day 82

Conquer Yourself

Day 83

Conquer Yourself

Day 84

Conquer Yourself

Day 85

Conquer Yourself

Day 86

Conquer Yourself

Day 87

Conquer Yourself

Day 88

Day 89

Day 90

Day 91

Conquer Yourself

Day 92

Day 93

Conquer Yourself

Day 94

Conquer Yourself

Day 95

Upon achieving goals, it becomes easy to digress.
How are you staying focused?

Conquer Yourself

"YOU MUST TELL YOURSELF, NO MATTER HOW HARD IT GETS, I'M GOING TO MAKE IT."

-Les Brown

"WHAT KIND OF COMPETITOR SEES THE FINISH LINE AND SLOWS DOWN...ALWAYS FINISH STRONG."

-Gary Ryan Blair

Day 96

Conquer Yourself

Day 97

Conquer Yourself

Day 98

Conquer Yourself

Day 99

Conquer Yourself

Day 100

Conquer Yourself

Day 101

Conquer Yourself

Day 102

Conquer Yourself

Day 103

Conquer Yourself

Day 104

Day 105

Day 106

Conquer Yourself

Day 107

Conquer Yourself

Day 108

Day 109

Conquer Yourself

Day 110

Conquer Yourself

Day 111

Conquer Yourself

Day 112

Conquer Yourself

Day 113

Day 114

Day 115

Conquer Yourself

Plate 116

"LIFE IS NOT ABOUT WINNING THE RACE. LIFE IS ABOUT FINISHING THE RACE."

-Marc Mero

YOUR JOURNEY IS
COMING TO AN END!
ITS TIME TO
REFLECT ON HOW FAR
YOU'VE COME AND
DETERMINE
HOW MUCH SELF
DISCIPLINE YOU'VE
GAINED.

Day 116

My proudest accomplishments on this journey. . .

Home Stretch

Day 116

Home Stretch

Day 116

Home Stretch

Day 117

Now that you've formed new habits,
how will you continue to maintain them?

Maintain to Sustain

Day 117

Maintain to Sustain

Day 118

Now that you've broken old habits,
how will you stay away from them?

Gone & Forgotten

Day 118

Gone & Forgotten

Day 119

Take a moment to celebrate your new found discipline.
Use the affirmations below to help you continue to
prosper on your self discipline path.

I am capable of keeping the promises I make to myself.

I am disciplined enough to achieve my goals.

I am responsible for all of my success.

I approach the day with enthusiam.

I use my energy to focus on my goals.

I have the self control to stay disciplined with my desires.

I am a champion of self discipline.

It feels good to be accomplishing my goals.

I feel satistfied when I work on my self.

Day 120

CERTIFICATE OF

DISCIPLINE

YOU'VE MADE IT TO THE FINAL DAY! THE JOURNEY DOESN'T END HERE. TAKE EVERYTHING YOU'VE LEARNED AND COMMIT TO A LIFE OF DISCIPLINE.